RL 9.2
pts 2

CUTTING EDGE MEDICINE

Genetics in Medicine

Andrew Solway

WORLD ALMANAC® LIBRARY

Please visit our Web site at: **www.garethstevens.com**
For a free color catalog describing World Almanac® Library's list of high-quality books
and multimedia programs, call 1-800-848-2928 (USA) or 1-800-387-3178 (Canada).
World Almanac® Library's fax: (414) 332-3567.

Library of Congress Cataloging-in-Publication Data available upon request from publisher.
Fax (414) 336-0157 for the attention of the Publishing Records Department.

ISBN 978-0-8368-7865-3 (lib. bdg.)

This North American edition first published in 2007 by
World Almanac® Library
A Member of the WRC Media Family of Companies
330 West Olive Street, Suite 100
Milwaukee, WI 53212 USA

This U.S. edition copyright © 2007 by World Almanac® Library.
Original edition copyright © 2007 by Arcturus Publishing Limited.

Produced by Arcturus Publishing Limited.
Editor: Alex Woolf
Designer: Nick Phipps
Consultant: Dr. Eleanor Clarke

World Almanac® Library editor: Carol Ryback
World Almanac® Library designer: Kami M. Strunsee
World Almanac® Library art direction: Tammy West
World Almanac® Library production: Jessica Yanke and Robert Kraus

The right of Andrew Solway to be identified as the author of this work has been
asserted by him in accordance with the Copyright, Designs and Patents Act, 1988.

Photo credits: Rex: /Sunset 52. Science Photo Library: /Bluestone 5, 58; /Pasieka 7; /D. Phillips 8;
/A. Barrington Brown 10; /LTH NHS Trust/Tim Vernon 13; /Laguna Design 15, 21; /Eye of Science 17, 27;
/ISM 18; /ISM/J. C. Revy 22; /Volker Steger 25; /Pascal Goetgheluck 28, 31; /David Scharf 32; /Eurelios
/P. Plailly 35, 39; /Gary Parker 36; /James King-Holmes 40; /Hybrid Medical Animation 43;
/Geoff Tompkinson 45; /Andrew Leonard 47; /Antonia Reeve 48; /Pasquale Sorrentino 50;
/Professors P. Motta and T. Naguro 54; /David Parker 57.

Printed in China

1 2 3 4 5 6 7 8 9 10 10 09 08 07 06

Contents

CHAPTER 1

What Is Genetics?

G enetics is the science of heredity—the similarities and differences that pass between generations (from parents to offspring) of humans, other animals, and plants. Genetics involves the study of genes, the tiny biological blueprints of life that make us human or grow an oak tree from an acorn. The fascinating science of genetics includes research into how genes work and what controls them, the discovery of the links between genetics and diseases, and how we use genetic information to understand and improve our quality of life.

The science of genetics is less than two hundred years old, but it has become a powerful tool in medicine. Genetic techniques have advanced to the point where the creation of clones—exact genetic copies—of many existing plants or animals is a reality. Our knowledge of genetics may one day enable us to grow entire human organs to replace those that are failing, damaged, or genetically faulty.

Although genetics holds great promise for future medical advancements, it also raises troubling questions. Is it right to select the genes of an unborn child in order to create a "designer baby" with a desired body shape, eye color, or level of intelligence? What

CUTTING EDGE   SCIENCE

What is a cell?

A cell is the smallest complete unit of a living organism. Every cell is a highly organized structure within a definite border—either a cell membrane (in animals) or a cell wall (in plants)—that includes the cytoplasm, or main body of the cell, and a "command center," or nucleus. The nucleus also contains a complete copy of that organism's genetic information.

All living things are made up of cells. Micro-organisms, such as bacteria, are single cells. An adult human, on the other hand, contains about 100 trillion cells. The nucleus of nearly every human cell contains a dark material called chromatin, which forms into rod-shaped structures called chromosomes during cell division. Each chromosome contains hundreds of genes.

will happen if we come to depend on herds of cloned animals for food? How will our ability to predict what diseases people might get or how long they will live affect our everyday lives? What safety precautions are in place to prevent genes from one species accidentally transferring to another species? Perhaps the biggest question of all is: Who decides where we draw the line concerning the use of genetic procedures?

A great grandmother (*right*) with her daughter, granddaughter, and great-granddaughter. The four share many genes that result in similar physical traits.

What are genes?

Genes are what make every living thing look and behave as it does. All the genes in a cell or organism are collectively known as a genome. We receive our genes from our parents. What determines who gets which genes? What information do they carry, and how do they carry it?

DNA, chromosomes and genes

Every cell in your body (except for mature red blood cells) holds within it the key to your genetic information, or genome. Most of the time, this genetic material is present in the cell's nucleus as an unordered substance called chromatin. When the cell begins to divide, however, the chromatin assembles itself into doubled strands called chromosomes. These chromosomes consist of long twisted molecules of deoxyribonucleic acid (DNA). Definite, orderly sections of the DNA are called genes. Each gene contains hundreds of linked subunits known as nucleotides.

CUTTING EDGE MOMENTS

Counting chromosomes

Chromosomes are hard to study because they only show clearly during cell division. In 1956, Swedish geneticists Joe Hin Tjio and Albert Levan dicovered a way to "freeze" cell division at a certain point and separate the chromosomes. They were the first scientists to accurately count the number of chromosomes in each human cell: Forty-six.

Each nucleotide, in turn, consists of three parts: a sugar molecule, a chemical called a phosphate group, and a chemical called a base. There are four bases—adenine (A), thymine (T), cytosine (C), and guanine (G). The bases always link the same way: A always links to T; C always links to G.

In order to understand how the nucleotide sections join to form genes, we need to consider the twisted ladder structure of the DNA molecule itself. A pair of bases (A–T or C–G) connects to form a horizontal "rung" of the DNA ladder, while the sugar molecule and phosphate group link to form the two sides that make up the "backbone" of the DNA ladder. A designated section of the DNA

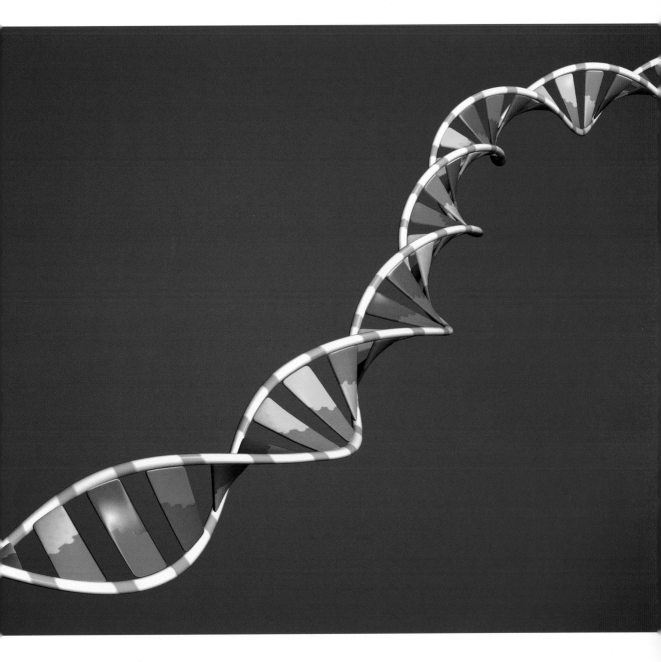

ladder with a specific arrangement of the bases is considered a gene. The average length of each gene is about three thousand nucleotide subunits.

Like the body cells themselves, DNA molecules have mastered the mathematical trick of multiplying by dividing. During a series of steps called mitosis (normal cell division), each chromosomal strand of DNA in the original "parent" cell splits apart down the middle of its "rungs."

A simplified model of part of a DNA molecule. The two white and orange rods indicate the sugar-phosphate backbone, while the flat red, blue, green, and yellow "rungs" indicate the base pairs.

During mitosis, a free-floating base within the nucleus pairs up with its complementary base on an open DNA strand to create a copy of the original chromosome. The copied strand is identical to the original. As the cell continues its division of the nucleus and cytoplasm, one full set of forty-six chromosomes—complete with all the genetic instructions (DNA) for that organism—moves into the nucleus within each new cell.

A different type of cell division, called meiosis, produces gametes (female egg cells and male sperm cells)—the cells involved with human reproduction. Meiosis includes a second cell division

A scanning electron micrograph (a photo taken through a scanning electron microscope) shows human sperm cells surrounding an egg cell. Only one sperm will fertilize the egg.

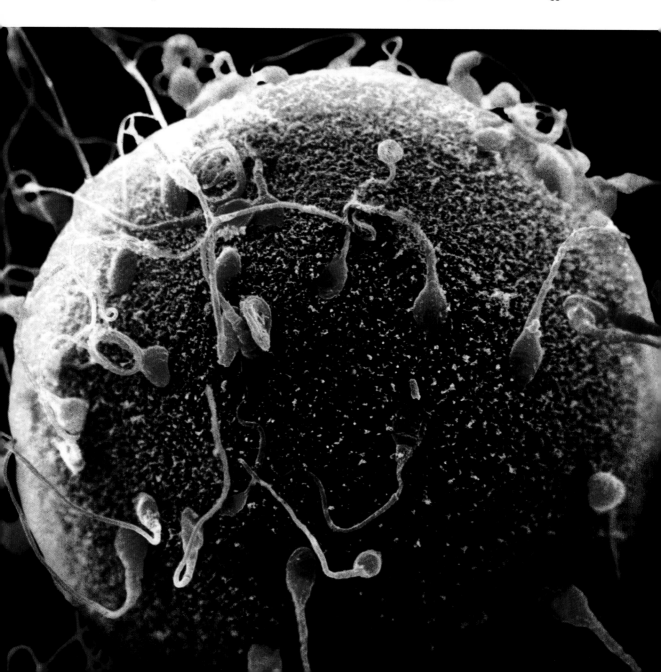

that produces cells with only twenty-three chromosomes, half the normal number of chromosomes found in regular body cells. While meiosis follows the same basic replication steps as mitosis, in meiotic cell division, when the chromosomes split to replicate, they also exchange some genes. Two new cells form. Cell division continues in the new cells, and each pair of chromosomes splits again, but they do not replicate. Instead, a single set of chromosomes end up in each of the four new cells. These new cells contain only half of the genes (DNA) of the original parent cell.

CUTTING EDGE SCIENCE

Giant molecules

A molecule is a collection of different atoms joined together. Some substances have small molecules made of just a few atoms. Water molecules, for instance, contain just three atoms. Many substances found in living organisms have much larger molecules consisting of hundreds or thousands of atoms. DNA molecules are truly enormous. They can contain millions—or even billions—of atoms.

Specks of life

Human egg cells measure about one-tenth of a millimeter across. Sperm cells are much smaller—about five microns (five twenty-five-thousandths of an inch) long. These two tiny specks may unite. Each gamete contributes half the genes (and, therefore, half the DNA) needed to form a completely new human. The sperm cell contains genes (DNA) from the father, and the egg cell carries genes (DNA) from the mother.

During sexual reproduction, the father's sperm cells pass into the mother's body, where egg and sperm meet to combine genetic information. In this way, genes from each parent pass from one generation (the parents) to the next (the offspring). Only one sperm cell combines with, or fertilizes, an egg cell. This fertilized cell, or zygote, is the first cell of what will become a human being. While still small and growing inside its mother, this mass of cells is called a blastocyst—which soon becomes an embryo.

The embryo grows through many stages of cell division. After a certain size, the embryo becomes a fetus, which grows into a baby.

James Watson (*left*) and Francis Crick with their model of the DNA molecule.

Genes and proteins

The genes that make up our chromosomes carry information about how to make proteins. A protein molecule consists of a long chain of smaller units called amino acids that are linked end to end. Twenty amino acids form all the different proteins.

Genes carry instructions for the order of the amino acids in each protein chain. Even a small change in the arrangement of amino acids in a protein can prevent that protein from doing its job. The order of base pairs of the DNA in the gene forms a code that the cell "reads" to make a particular protein.

Proteins have two major functions in the body. They make up most of the structure of certain body parts, such as muscles. Proteins also control metabolism—the processes going on in the body, such as digesting food.

CUTTING EDGE MOMENTS

Watson, Crick, Franklin, and Wilkins

Four people—James Watson, Francis Crick, Rosalind Franklin, and Maurice Wilkins—discovered the structure of DNA in 1953. X-ray "pictures" of DNA taken by Franklin and Wilkins revealed vital information about the shape of the DNA molecule and its size. Watson and Crick, working in Cambridge, England, determined the final details of DNA structure using a large 3-D "modeling kit."

Making a protein

Proteins are not produced in the nucleus, where all the cell's genetic material is found. Instead, they are made in structures called ribosomes located in the cytoplasm, or main part of the cell. A special "messenger" substance called messenger ribonucleic acid, or mRNA, carries the instructions for making a particular protein from the nucleus to the ribosome. RNA is similar to DNA, but has a slightly different nucleotide base (uracil instead of thymine). Messenger RNA is one of several types of RNA. Like the genes in the nucleus, mRNA carries protein instructions in an orderly arrangement of base pairs along its length.

The mRNA links up with a ribosome in the cytoplasm. The ribosome "reads" the coded information carried by the mRNA and produces the protein, one amino acid at a time.

CHAPTER 2

From Genes to Characteristics

We know that genes are made of DNA and that they contain the information for making proteins. But how does this account for everything that genes do? Genes make us what we are. They control how a fertilized human egg grows to become a baby instead of a kitten or an oak sapling. Genes are also the reason for many of the differences between people. If someone has blue eyes and blond hair, these characteristics come from the person's genes.

Genes produce all these effects through proteins. Our eye color and hair color, for instance, depend on chemicals called pigments. Proteins called enzymes control the processes that produce these different pigments.

Different genes

More than 99.9 percent of genes are exactly the same in all people. These are the genes that make us human beings. The other 0.1 percent of genes are the ones that make people different from each other. For instance, six genes produce proteins that affect eye color. Not everyone has the same version of each of these genes. Different versions of the same gene are known as alleles. Depending on which alleles a person has, his or her eyes can be any color—from light gray to dark brown.

CUTTING EDGE — FACTS

Human DNA

- Human DNA consists of 23 pairs of chromosomes, made up of about 3 billion genes.
- Each cell holds about 3 feet (1 meter) of coiled-up DNA. If all the DNA in your body were stretched out, it would reach to the Sun and back at least six hundred times.
- About 95 percent of human DNA occurs in long stretches of repeating base sequences of "junk DNA" that are not part of any gene. Yeast and bacteria do not contain any "junk DNA."
- Human DNA contains about 30,000 genes. Scientists have identified about half of them.

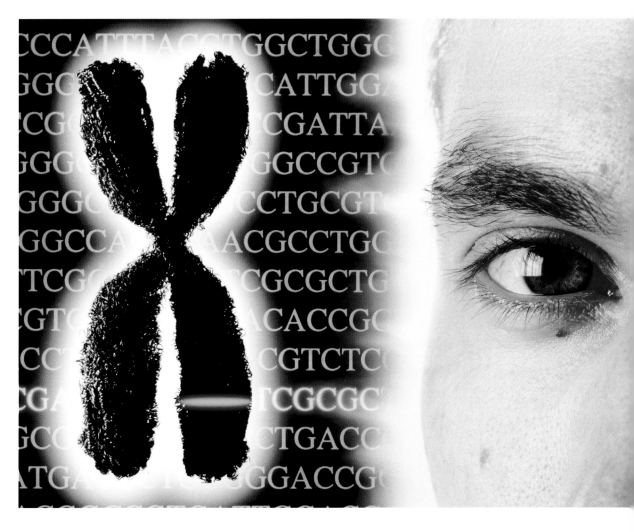

Two of everything

Like a deck of cards, the human genome is "shuffled" every time a new egg and sperm meet. Humans normally inherit two copies of each gene, carried on forty-six chromosomes. One chromosome comes from each parent. No one can predict exactly which genes will pass to the next generation. Sometimes, genetic traits seem to skip a generation and an offspring bears an almost stronger resemblance to one of its grandparents than to its parents. Other times, the same two parents may produce one child with brown hair and brown eyes, while a second child is blond and blue-eyed.

Your genome is your genotype: the genes you carry in every cell. Unless you are an identical twin, your genotype is uniquely your own. Your phenotype—what you look like—is the physical expression of those genes and your environment.

A computer-generated illustration shows a chromosomal pair and a person with brown eyes. The highlighted area on the chromosome and the letters of genetic code next to it represent the genes for eye color. Brown eyes are dominant over blue. Two brown-eyed parents who both carry a recessive gene allele for blue eyes can produce a blue-eyed baby if they both pass that recessive allele to their offspring.

13

Genes on and off

Some genes are essential to all cells and are active most of the time. Genes that make the proteins that produce energy in the cell are active most of the time. Most genes, however, are only active at certain times or in certain cells. For example, in young red blood cells, the genes that produce the protein hemoglobin (which carries oxygen in the blood) are switched on. By contrast, in hair cells in the skin, the genes for hemoglobin are turned off, while the genes that produce the protein keratin (the protein from which hair is made) are switched on.

We have two copies of every gene. How do they work together to give us our physical characteristics? In the nineteenth century, a Czech monk named Gregor Mendel discovered what became the basic rules for genetic inheritance. Ironically, Mendel knew nothing about DNA or genes—but he knew a lot about plants.

CUTTING EDGE   SCIENTISTS

Gregor Mendel (1822–1884)

Gregor Mendel began training as a monk at St. Thomas's monastery in what is now Brno, Czech Republic, when he was twenty-one. He was interested in the sciences, especially botany, and in his mid-twenties he spent two years at the University of Vienna, Austria, studying natural sciences (biology) and math. Mendel concentrated on studying why two strong and vigorous plants can produce offspring that do not always exhibit the same qualities as the parent plants. Although Mendel's research did not solve this problem, it signaled the beginning of the science of genetics.

Mendelian genetics

Mendel conducted thousands of experiments over the many years he spent studying how pea plants inherited different characteristics. For example, Mendel bred together a pea plant with purple flowers and one with white flowers. The plants that grew from this combination all produced purple flowers. Mendel then took these plants and bred them together. The next generation (the offspring of the purple-flowered plants) produced a mixture of white-and purple-flowered plants, which appeared in a consistent ratio: three purple-flowered plants to every one white-flowered plant.

Modern explanations

The ideas that Mendel suggested to explain his results formed the basis of modern genetics. He proposed that the parent plants each contributed one "unit of inheritance" to their offspring for each characteristic. Mendel also said that in any pair of characteristics, one of the two has more influence, or is "dominant," while the other is "recessive." A dominant characteristic, or trait, is one that

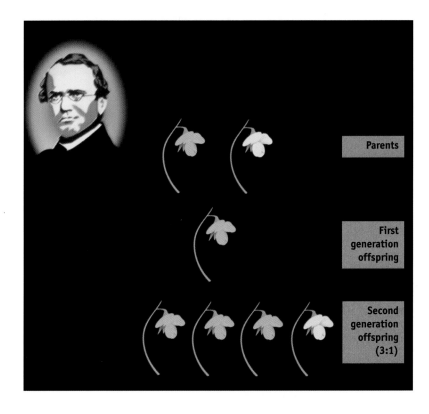

Parents

First generation offspring

Second generation offspring (3:1)

Gregor Mendel demonstrated that one of the genes that determined the color of pea plant flowers was dominant over another. When a white- and a purple-flower pea plant were bred together, all the offspring had purple flowers because the purple-flower gene was dominant. The white-flower gene was not lost— it appeared again in the next generation.

appears physically, even when it is inherited only from one parent. A recessive trait does not appear in an offspring unless inherited from both parents (*see chart, page 16*).

What Mendel called dominant and recessive characteristics are actually different alleles (types) of the same gene. In Mendel's experiments, the purple-flower allele was the dominant phenotype, and the white flower allele was recessive. Purple-flowered plants had two dominant purple-flower alleles (labeled PP), while the white-flowered plants had two resessive white-flower alleles (pp). All the offspring had one allele from each parent: Their genotype was Pp. All the plants from that generation produced purple flowers.

Mendel also concluded that it was a matter of chance as to which alleles were passed to offspring. An example of how this works is displayed in the second part of Mendel's experiment (*right*). Each first-generation plant had two possible alleles: purple flower (P) or white flower (p). The table shows four possible combinations of these two alleles. Three combinations—PP, Pp, pP—produce purple flowers. One combination—pp—produces white flowers. Since Mendel found experimentally that he grew three purple flowers for every one white flower, it suggests that there are equal chances for each combination of alleles to occur.

Not always simple

Mendel devised some clear rules about the inheritance of simple, contrasting characteristics, such as purple and white flowers. Not all characteristics are inherited in such a simple way, however. For instance, one allele is not always dominant over another. Snapdragons can have red flowers or white flowers, but they can also have pink flowers. Pink-flower snapdragons have one white-flower allele and one red-flower allele. Neither of the two alleles is dominant.

The biggest complication of inheritance in humans is that hardly any characteristics are inherited through a single gene. Eye color, for

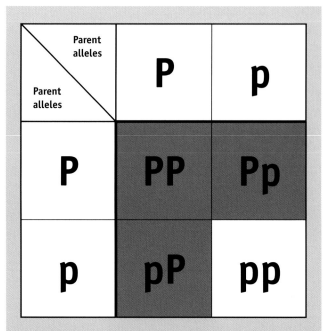

The upper row and left-hand column of this table represent the different alleles of the parent plants. The four boxes in the lower right-hand area represent the possible combinations of the parent alleles in the offspring. The purple-shaded boxes show the combinations that produce purple flowers, and the white box shows the combination that produces white flowers.

CUTTING EDGE   SCIENCE

Errors in DNA replication

DNA is programmed to copy itself. Every time a cell divides, the chromosomal strands of DNA molecules "unzip," and bases that float freely in the nucleus join to their "unzipped" complement to help form a new chromosomal strand. All the genetic material in the nucleus is thus copied. DNA replication (copying) is a mostly error-free process, but a copying error occurs in every three or four cell divisions. If a copying error gets into a gamete, it passes to the next generation. Usually, the error results in a defective gene which may cause disease or death. Occasionally, however, a genetic error causes an advantage, such as immunity to (the ability to resist) a disease (*see pages 26–28*).

example, involves at least six different genes. Other characteristics, such as height, are the result of the interaction of many genes.

Other factors can affect physical characteristics and behavior. Environmental and nutritional circumstances also influence development. Children exposed to lead in the air or mercury in the water will suffer adverse effects. A child's development is also strongly affected by what his or her mother eats during pregnancy as well as the nutritional quality of that person's childhood diet.

Fruit flies reproduce quickly and are widely used for genetic research. They have unusual DNA in their salivary glands—the genes appear as dark and light bands. A DNA copying error (mutation) in the DNA of this fruit fly caused it to grow two pairs of wings instead of one.

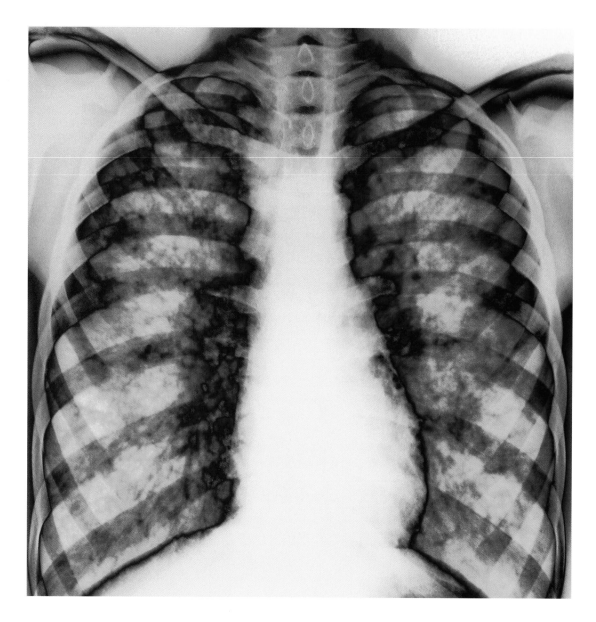

Genotype versus phenotype

In 1990, the Human Genome Project began. Its goal was to determine the sequence (order) of the entire human genome. This mammoth task was completed in 2003. As a result, we now know the order of all three billion base pairs in human DNA. Genes that hold codes for proteins make up only about 5 percent of the sequence; the rest is "junk" DNA that does not code for proteins. Scientists know what about half of the thirty thousand or so genes do. It will take many years to discover what every gene does.

A colored X-ray of the chest of someone with cystic fibrosis, an inherited disease that causes an overproduction of mucus in the lungs. The darker blue color in the X-ray shows the thick mucus buildup caused by the disease.

Introducing variety

In humans, the only characteristics that have been found to be controlled by a single gene are certain hereditary (genetic) disorders (disorders that are passed on through the genes from one generation to the next). Hereditary disorders result when a parent passes his or her mutated gene to an offspring. A new genetic mutation can also occur during meiosis. Mutations occur randomly and naturally. Non-genetic factors, such as exposure to toxic chemicals or radiation, can also cause changes in genes.

Changes to the DNA sometimes cause problems that make a person less fit and healthy. Some mutations prove beneficial. For instance, some people carry a mutated gene that causes a lack of a certain protein on the surface of their cells. People with this mutated gene do not develop HIV/AIDS. Such beneficial mutations not only promote genetic diversity between humans, but also ultimately support the huge variety of organisms living on Earth.

CUTTING EDGE FACTS

Some common genetic disorders

These are just a few of the 10,000 or so known genetic disorders:

Alzheimer's disease A brain disorder that causes people to slowly lose their memory and their ability to write or even speak. The disease most commonly affects elderly people.

Cystic fibrosis A disease in which thick, sticky mucus clogs the lungs and digestive tract.

Duchenne muscular dystrophy and Becker muscular dystrophy Types of muscle-wasting diseases.

Hemophilia A and B Blood disorders that prevent the blood from clotting properly; the slightest cut causes serious bleeding.

Phenylketonuria One of the most common inherited disorders. It causes serious brain damage if not identified. Babies are tested for the disease at birth. People who have the disorder must eat a low-protein diet to live normally.

Sickle cell anemia A blood cell disorder caused by an error in the structure of hemoglobin (the protein that carries oxygen in the blood). Sickle cell affects the shape of the red blood cells and interfers with the blood's ability to carry oxygen around the body. The misshapen sickle cells can also cause blood clots (*see also pages 26–28*).

CHAPTER 3

Genetic Engineering

Genetic engineering involves making changes to the DNA of an organism. It includes engineering new kinds of species and cloning—making exact genetic copies—of plants or animals. Genetic engineering usually involves adding or replacing genes in eggs or developing embryos. Scientists have developed a range of tools to study and manipulate genes.

Some uses of genetic engineering are controversial. Many people feel that putting genetic material from one organism into another is morally wrong and could even be dangerous, because genes transferred from another species may have unexpected effects. In most countries, strict rules that include descriptions of safe and acceptable techniques govern genetic research.

Genetic engineering techniques are very useful in medicine. They are mainly used to produce medically useful substances, such as hormones (naturally produced chemical "messengers" that travel through the blood and affect various body organs or processes) and antibodies (special proteins that help the body's immune system fight diseases).

Genetic enzymes

Enzymes play an important role in genetic engineering techniques. Enzymes are proteins that control chemical reactions in the body. They are catalysts: Enzymes speed up chemical reactions without becoming a part of the reaction.

CUTTING EDGE   FACTS

Rearranging DNA molecules

Scientists use two types of enzymes, restriction enzymes and DNA ligases, as tools to rearrange DNA molecules. Restriction enzymes, produced by bacteria, detect the order of the base pairs on a strand of DNA and then select, or cut out, that specific area, leaving exposed "sticky ends." DNA ligases cause the exposed sticky ends of DNA molecules to reattach, forming an unbroken new strand of DNA.

Enzymes catalyze every metabolic process throughout the body.

DNA polymerase was one of the first genetic enzymes discovered. In order for DNA to copy itself, the DNA molecule must "unzip." DNA polymerase is the enzyme that causes the "unzipping" of DNA. As the free-floating bases in the nucleus find their complement, a new, duplicate DNA strand forms. With the help of DNA polymerase and other enzymes, researchers can build their own DNA molecules in a test tube and make copies of a piece of DNA.

Scientists can also "cut and paste" sections of DNA together using another group of enzymes called restriction enzymes. These enzymes act as biological "knives" to cut, or isolate, smaller chunks of the DNA molecule. Restriction enzymes cut one side of a DNA molecule in a specific place and the other side of the molecule in another place, several base pairs away, leaving an uneven section of DNA known as a "sticky end." If a different molecule of DNA is cut with the same restriction enzyme, another sticky end of DNA forms. An enzyme called DNA ligase joins together the two pieces of sticky ended DNA to form a piece of recombined ("recombinant") DNA.

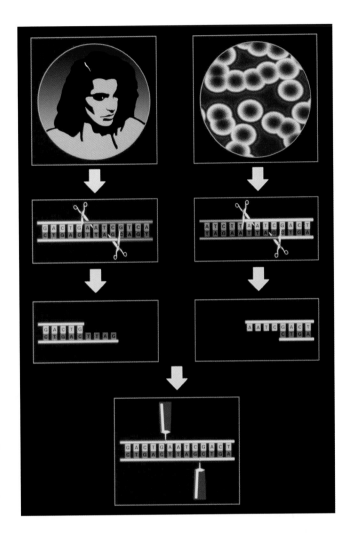

A restriction enzyme (shown as the scissors) cuts human DNA and bacterial DNA. The two cut pieces of DNA have "sticky ends" that can be joined using the enzyme DNA ligase (shown as tubes of glue) to form a new strand of recombined DNA, often called recombinant DNA.

Protein factories

The discovery of genetic enzymes made genetic engineering possible. The most successful use of genetic engineering to date has involved using bacteria and other microbes to produce medically useful proteins. In other words, these microorganisms have become living, protein-producing "factories."

Finding the right gene

The fact that all organisms share a certain amount of DNA allows the use of microbes to produce needed human proteins. Insulin and growth hormone, for instance, do not need to be produced by mammals to work properly in mammals.

The first step in the process involves separating the human gene that directs the formation of ("codes for") the specific desired protein. Finding a particular gene often take years of research, but

A highly magnified microscope image of a plasmid (*see page 23*) shows a highlighted section (*green circle*) that was added using genetic engineering techniques.

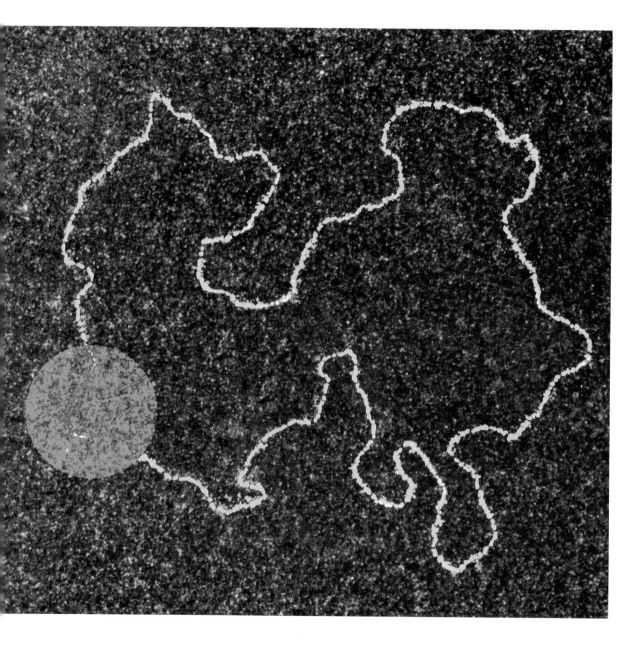

CUTTING EDGE   SCIENCE

Making human insulin

Insulin is a hormone (a "messenger" protein) that circulates in the blood and affects cells around the body. Insulin enables the body to absorb glucose (a type of sugar that functions as the main fuel for body cells) from the blood. Diabetics—people with diabetes—cannot make enough of their own insulin. They need regular insulin injections to regulate their blood sugar. In the past, this insulin came from pigs, but pig insulin is not exactly the same as human insulin, so it sometimes caused problems. It was also expensive to produce.

Genetic engineering makes possible the production of human insulin using bacteria. Scientists incorporated the human gene for making the insulin protein into bacteria. Huge numbers of bacteria are grown in large fermenters (big tanks used for growing microorganisms). They produce substantial amounts of human insulin.

once scientists identify the gene, they can separate it from the surrounding DNA using restriction enzymes. What's left is a piece of DNA with sticky end that carries a specific human gene.

Using plasmids

After the scientists isolate the desired human gene, they need to transport it into a bacterial cell. Structures called plasmids—small, circular or irregularly shaped molecules of DNA found naturally in many bacteria—provide an excellent means of transporting genes. A plasmid usually contains a gene or genes that give the bacteria a useful characteristic. For instance, a plasmid could contain the gene or genes for making an enzyme that helps a bacterium defend itself against some viruses. Bacteria can pass plasmids between themselves. They also copy the plasmids along with the rest of their DNA when they reproduce.

Scientists often use plasmids to transport human DNA into bacteria. Using the same basic procedures as those for making recombinant DNA, scientists cut the plasmid with a restriction enzyme and turn it into a straight piece of DNA with sticky ends. Then they attach the human DNA (which also has sticky ends) to the plasmid's DNA. A plasmid containing DNA from different sources is known as a recombinant plasmid.

Researchers mix the recombinant plasmids with bacteria. The bacteria incorporate the plasmids—some of which contain the human gene—and production of the required protein begins.

Medically useful products

Human insulin, which is used to treat diabetes, was the first medically useful protein produced by genetic engineering (GE) techniques (*see sidebar, page 23*). Genetically engineered human insulin was approved for use in humans in 1982. Since then, similar GE techniques have helped produce many other proteins. For instance, blood clotting proteins that treat the genetic disorder hemophilia, in which the blood does not clot properly, are produced using GE techniques.

Another genetically engineered protein, erythropoietin, causes the production of red blood cells. Erythropoietin is used to treat anemia, a condition in which there are too few red blood cells.

Several proteins that stimulate the immune system (the body's system of defending itself against disease) are also produced by genetic engineering. They are used as vaccines to prevent diseases such as viral hepatitis (a serious liver disease).

Yeasts and cell cultures

One problem with using plasmids to carry genetically engineered material into bacterial cells is that plasmids can only carry small chunks of DNA. Some genes, or groups of genes, are too large to be incorporated into a plasmid. Since the 1980s, yeasts (a more complex microbe) and cell cultures ("colonies" of human or animal cells grown in the laboratory) have also been genetically modified and used as protein factories.

CUTTING EDGE   SCIENCE

What is a cell culture?

A cell culture is a colony (cluster) of cells from a human or animal that are grown in the laboratory under carefully controlled conditions, either as single layers of cells on a glass or plastic surface or suspended (dispersed) in a liquid. One problem with many types of cell cultures is that they die after 50 to 100 divisions. A few types, however, are "immortal"—they continue dividing indefinitely. One of the most useful immortal stem cell lines (called "CHO") comes from the ovaries of Chinese hamsters.

A scientist purifies human insulin produced by genetically engineered yeast. Insulin is separated from the yeast cells inside this large container.

CHAPTER 4

Genetic Disorders

Medical researchers have made tremendous advances in the study of genetic disorders. From among the thousands of genes in the human genome, they have pinpointed individual genes that cause genetic disorders and have isolated the proteins produced by these genes.

How genetic disorders are passed on

A change in just one gene can cause a genetic disorder. Most genes that cause such disorders are recessive traits, like the white flowers in Mendel's pea plant experiments (*see pages 15–17*). Only those who inherit two alleles (copies) of the "faulty" gene develop a genetic disorder. Someone who inherits only one of the faulty genes also carries a normal, dominant allele, and does not develop the disease. A person with the recessive gene can, however, pass the disease to offspring if his or her partner carries the recessive gene.

People with genetic disorders often die in childhood. They do not survive to reproduce and cannot pass on their genes to the next generation. A "carrier" with the recesssive gene can, however, enjoy a normal life span and produce children. Genetic disorders generally pass from one generation to the next through carriers and not those who actually develop the disease.

Sickle cell anemia

Most genetic disorders cause health problems. Sickle cell anemia is a genetic disorder that affects hemoglobin, the protein that allows red blood cells (RBCs) to carry oxygen through the body. People with sickle cell anemia produce abnormal hemoglobin. The RBCs become sickle-shaped (crescent-shaped) and "sticky." This stickiness causes the sickled RBCs to clump together and block blood vessels. The RBCs also break apart easily, which causes anemia (abnormally low RBC levels in the blood).

In 1956, sickle cell anemia became the first genetic disease that scientists could identify genetically. They found that one misplaced amino acid on a certain gene caused people to develop the disease.

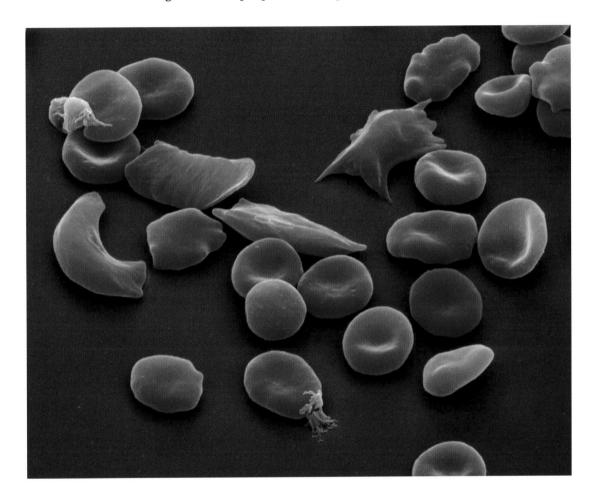

The blood of people with sickle cell anemia contains normal (disk-shaped) red blood cells as well as the curved and distorted blood cells (pinkish) typical of sickle cell anemia.

CUTTING EDGE **SCIENCE**

Sickle cell genes

People with two sickle cell alleles usually endure ill health and often die young of a heart attack. The disease stresses the heart, which strains to push the sticky sickle cells through blood vessels. Other organs, such as the kidneys, are affected as well. People who carry only one sickle cell allele suffer only mild symptoms of the disease.

Mosquitos spread malaria—a major, worldwide disease that kills at least one million annually throughout tropical countries. Sickle-shaped RBCs prevent the malaria parasite from reproducing. People who develop sickle cell anemia, therefore, develop a "natural immunity" to malaria. Ironically, those who develop sickle cell anemia sometimes survive malaria and pass on their defective gene.

An eight-cell embryo produced by in vitro fertilization (fertilization in a test tube) is tested for genetic disorders before transfer to the mother's body.

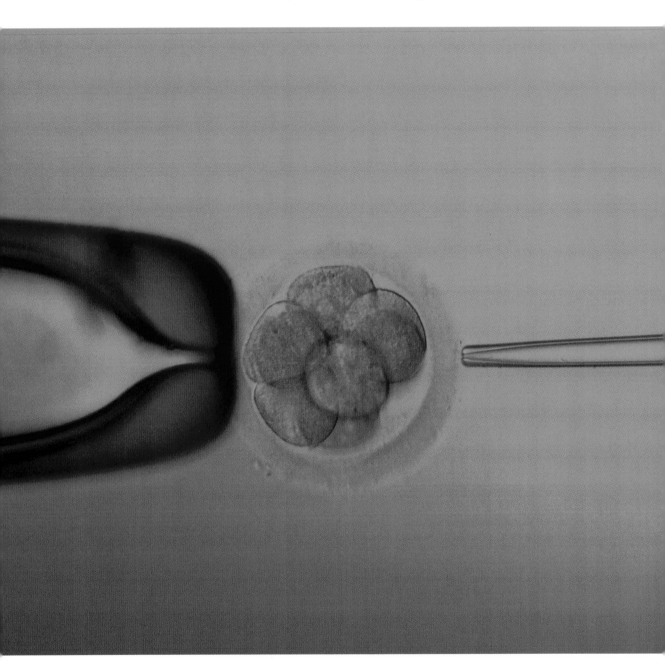

Genetic testing

Once scientists identify a gene that causes a hereditary disorder, testing others for that gene is relatively easy. People who might be carriers (for instance, somone whose relatives have the disorder) can have a blood test for that disease before they marry. If both partners carry the gene for the disease, they may consider how it could affect any children they may have. Each child of that couple would have a one-in-four chance of developing the disease. Testing blood from a newborn-baby's heel (known as the heel-prick test) can reveal genetic problems.

One genetic test developed in the 1990s hold much promise. About one in two hundred people in the United States carries a gene that can cause colon cancer when people reach middle-age. In the early 1990s, researchers discovered the faulty gene that causes the disease. Younger people whose family health history includes colon cancer can be tested for the faulty gene. Those found to carry it can eat a special diet that greatly reduces the chances of developing colon cancer.

Genetic testing for a disease is not always helpful. Alzheimer's disease is a genetic disorder that affects the brain. At first, it causes forgetfulness. In time, however, sufferers develop problems with speaking, understanding, reading, or writing. Alzheimer's does not usually affect people younger than sixty years of age. At present, Alzheimer's has no effective treatment or cure. Testing for Alzheimer's disease may do more harm than good. A person who knows his or her DNA can cause Alzheimer's disease may dread the future. That person may also develop anxieties or other psychological problems, such as depression.

CUTTING EDGE   MOMENTS

Genetic discrimination

Genetic discrimination means to treat someone unfairly because of their genetic makeup. Research published in Australia in 2005 suggests that genetic discrimination already occurs. In a study of one thousand Australians who were genetically tested for certain diseases, eighty-seven suffered some kind of discrimination as a result. For instance, one woman who carried genes that indicate a high risk of breast cancer was refused health insurance for any kind of cancer.

Genetic weaknesses

Disorders caused by single faulty genes were once thought to be the only kind of genetic disorder. Today, scientists have identified a genetic link to many common disorders, such as heart disease and cancer. In these cases, people are said to have a "genetic weakness." They carry particular alleles of one or more genes that make them more likely to develop a particular disease.

Having a genetic weakness does not always condemn that person to developing a particular disease. For instance, regular exercise and the adoption of a healthy diet can greatly reduce the chances of (or at least delay the development of) a genetic heart disease in someone whose genes are "against" him or her.

DNA microarrays

A new development in genetic testing—DNA microarrays (*see sidebar, below*)—makes it possible to test for thousands of genes at the same time. DNA microarrays could test for a wide range of genetic disorders or weaknesses. Such testing could offer tremendous benefits. People could be tested early in life, and doctors could advise them on what kind of diet and lifestyle would reduce the risks from their genetic weaknesses. Widespread genetic testing could also, however, lead to "genetic discrimination" (*see*

CUTTING EDGE   SCIENCE

DNA chips

DNA microarrays, also known as DNA "chips," are a fast and efficient way to perform thousands of genetic tests simultaneously. A DNA microarray is a flat plate that holds a number of known samples of DNA sequences (called probes) arranged in a grid. The probes consist of short pieces of DNA that link with "targets" in the test samples to identify a particular genetic disorder.

When someone's DNA is tested using a DNA chip, a sample of their DNA is broken up into small pieces, and the pieces are "labeled" with a fluorescent (glow-in-the-dark) dye. The DNA is then washed over the DNA microarray. If the person has a target section of DNA that matches one of the probes, that section binds to the DNA chip and shows up as a fluorescent dot. A technologist or doctor can identify the disorder from the position of the dot on the microarray.

sidebar, page 29). Employers might refuse to employ someone who has a strong risk of developing a particular disorder. Insurance companies might also refuse to insure people who have a high "genetic risk" of developing a serious illness.

A technolgist examines a DNA microarray that tests for many genetic abnormalities at once.

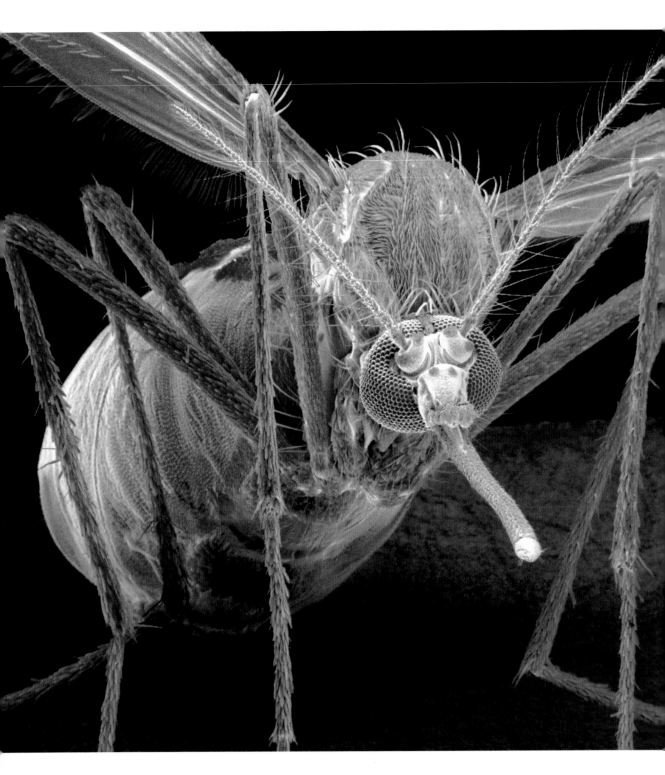

A vector is an agent that helps spread diseases by carrying viruses or bacteria. This mosquito is a "vector" for yellow fever, a viral disease. Researchers hope to use some genetically engineered viruses to help cure certain diseases.

Gene therapy

Gene therapy is an experimental medical technique that may eventually make it possible to cure people with genetic disorders. In gene therapy, doctors replace the "faulty" gene or genes with the normal gene or genes. Genetic engineering techniques permit the production of multiple copies of particular genes. The challenge comes in incorporating the normal copy of a gene or genes into the patient's DNA.

Since an adult human body has about one hundred trillion cells, inserting new DNA into every one of those cells is impossible. Most hereditary disorders affect particular areas of the body, however, so the new DNA must only reach those cells. Even so, transporting replacement genes into cells in a target area—much less getting the genes to work in the desired way—is extremely difficult.

Virus delivery

Viruses cannot copy their own DNA. They reproduce by moving into the cells of other "host" organisms and using the DNA of the host cell to reproduce. Viruses, therefore, can serve as the ideal carriers for transporting new genes into cells. Viruses used in gene therapy do not cause a severe reaction by the body's immune system. Scientists use modified human viruses—viruses that are genetically modified to carry certain genes but which do not themselves cause disease.

Some kinds of viruses naturally attack particular parts of the body and are used to deliver the gene therapy to a specific area. Adenoviruses, for instance, are a group of viruses that attack the nose, throat, lungs, or intestines. They are used in gene therapy that targets those areas.

CUTTING EDGE   SCIENCE

DNA nanoballs
A gene therapy method under development involves packing the genes into a tight ball and coating them with a protein layer. These particles, nicknamed "DNA nanoballs," are small enough to pass into the nucleus of a cell. The nanoballs are injected into the bloodstream, distributed around the body, and absorbed by the cells.

Non-viral carriers

In a number of cases, people who received gene therapy using viruses died or became ill (*see sidebar, below*). Researchers are now experimenting with new ways to transport genes into the cell. One technique involves removing cells from the patient, adding the new genes directly to the cells in the laboratory, and then transfusing the genetically engineered cells back into the patient.

Another technique uses small balls of lipids (natural oils or fats) known as liposomes. The replacement gene is placed inside the liposomes, which discharge the gene into the cytoplasm of a cell. Recently, researchers developed liposomes that deposit the gene into the cell's nucleus. Once in the nucleus, a replacement gene is likely to survive and be reproduced along with the original genes. Its effects should last longer than a gene inserted into the cytoplasm.

Problems and solutions

Gene therapy experiments (trials) on animals have been quite successful. In 2002, for instance, gene therapy was successfully used to correct sickle cell disease in mice. Human trials of gene therapies have had limited success, and there have been some serious setbacks (*see below*). Setbacks make researchers cautious about using gene therapy. At present, all gene therapies on humans are considered experimental and are being tested for safety.

CUTTING EDGE MOMENTS

Gene therapy failures

In 1999, eighteen-year-old Jesse Gelsinger, from Tucson, Arizona, participated in a gene therapy clinical trial (a test for new drugs or therapies) at the University of Pennsylvania in Philadelphia. Jesse had a genetic disorder that affected his liver and blood. The gene therapy was designed to cure the disease by inserting a new gene into liver cells. It used a virus to transport the gene.

Within hours of receiving the therapy, Jesse became very ill. His body's immune system reacted violently to the experimental treatment. Despite the best efforts of his doctors, Jesse died.

Since Jesse's death, several other people suffered ill effects of gene therapy treatment. These problems have made researchers reexamine their procedures for gene therapy.

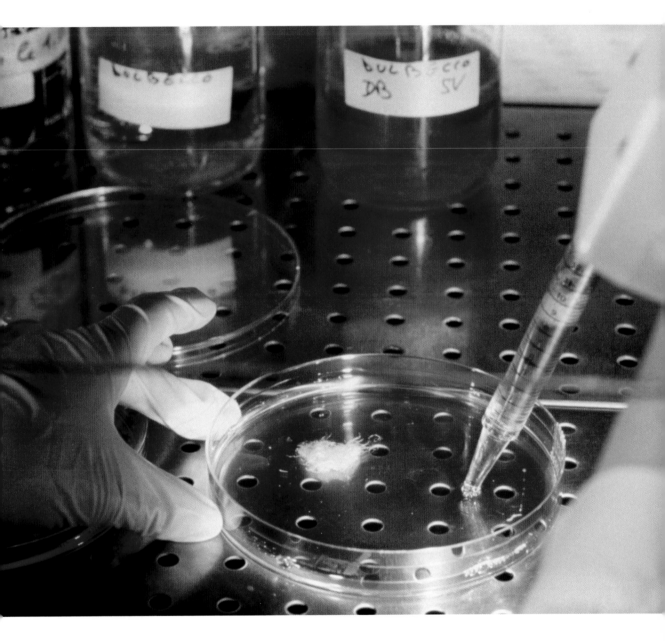

Despite the many problems, gene therapy still holds much promise for the treatment of a number of diseases. Researchers are exploring a new gene therapy technique that involves manipulating the cell's own DNA repair mechanisms to mend a faulty gene instead of replacing it altogether. The new technique eliminates the need to find a way of transporting new genes into the cells. Another advantage is that such a technique does not provoke an immune system reaction.

A scientist prepares a gene therapy implant for insertion into a patient. The implant consists of synthetic fibers mixed with genetically engineered cells.

CHAPTER 5

Cloning

A clone is a genetically identical copy of another animal or plant. A number of clones occur naturally. Identical twins are clones: They develop from the same fertilized egg. Some organisms, such as bacteria, yeasts, and other microbes, often clone themselves. They usually reproduce simply by dividing in two, then dividing again and again until there is a colony of billions—all genetically identical. Some of the more complex animals are also clones. Female aphids, for instance, produce thousands of young over the summer. All are genetically identical to the mother.

Early clones

German scientist Hans Spemann first proposed the idea of nuclear transfer cloning in 1938. He suggested taking a body cell from an adult organism, removing the nucleus, and putting it into an enucleated egg cell (one that has had its nucleus removed). In 1952,

Identical twins are natural clones. They form when an embryo splits in the early stages of development.

U.S. scientists Robert Briggs and Thomas J. King produced northern leopard frogs using Spemann's cloning method. Other groups of researchers cloned frogs of other species using the same techniques. British biologist John Gurdon cloned frogs and raised them to sexual maturity in 1962.

Scientists did not clone a mammal until the 1980s. In 1984, Danish scientist Steen Willadsen produced cloned sheep, and in 1985, he cloned cows by splitting very early embryos in half. This process is now usually called "twinning" instead of cloning. Twinning involves making twins from a naturally fertilized egg, while other forms of cloning use the body cells and unfertilized eggs of adult animals.

Transgenic animals

Transgenic animals are genetically engineered to contain a gene from a different animal species. Scientists wanted to refine cloning techniques as an easy, reliable way to produce transgenic farm animals that could produce human vaccines or other proteins in their milk. When a transgenic animal breeds normally, only half of the mother's genes pass to each of her offspring (*see page 9*). And, only some of those genes will be the engineered genes. Scientists hoped to use cloning to quickly produce large herds of transgenic animals, but they must also find a way to assure the inheritance of the engineered genes.

Scientists have produced transgenic animals using other techniques besides cloning. The earliest method involved injecting extra genes into a newly fertilized egg using a very fine syringe. This technique proved unreliable—only about 1 percent to 5 percent of the animals produced were transgenic. The reason for the low success rate is that the injection process often damages the nucleus and the genes inside it, so the egg does not develop.

Another technique uses a virus to carry extra genes into an egg cell, as in gene therapy. Scientists produced transgenic mice for research using this method.

CUTTING EDGE — SCIENCE

Glowing green mice

In 2002, a group of transgenic mice was engineered to glow bright green! The mice received a gene for a fluorescent (glow-in-the-dark) protein produced by jellyfish. The use of the fluorescent protein helped prove that the gene had been successfully incorporated into the mouse cells.

Three mothers

The first mammal cloned using DNA from a full-grown, adult animal was a sheep named Dolly. In a way, Dolly had three "mothers." Dolly's actual mother was a white-faced breed of sheep. All of Dolly's DNA came from this mother. Scientists took an udder cell from the white-faced sheep and grew it in the laboratory under special conditions.

Next, they took an egg cell from the second of Dolly's "mothers," a black-faced sheep. Scientists removed the nucleus of that egg cell and replaced it with the nucleus from the udder cell of the white-faced sheep. They used an electric shock to combine the cell and nucleus and make the two parts of the cell fuse (join) together. The electric shock also initiated cell division within the egg.

Once the scientists were sure that the egg was growing normally, they implanted it in the uterus of Dolly's third "mother," another black-faced female sheep. Dolly was born in July 1996. Her birth mother was a black-faced sheep, but Dolly's white face proved that she had the DNA of the white-faced sheep: Dolly was truly a clone.

Worldwide excitement

Dolly's birth was not made public until 1997, when the researchers were sure that she was developing normally. News of Dolly's arrival caused excitement around the world. There was talk of cloning beloved pets, or even successful people. With all the publicity surrounding Dolly, the original reason for her creation was

CUTTING EDGE   SCIENTISTS

Ian Wilmut (born 1944)

Ian Wilmut was the British scientist who led the research team that cloned Dolly the sheep. In 1973, while at Darwin College at the University of Cambridge in Cambridge, England, he created Frosty, the first calf grown from a frozen embryo. Wilmut moved to the Roslin Institute in Edinburgh, Scotland, in 1974. In early 1996, his research team cloned two sheep, Megan and Morag, from sheep embryo cells. Later that year, Wilmut's team cloned Dolly using DNA from an adult sheep. In 1997, his team produced a transgenic cloned sheep called Polly. Ian Wilmut is no longer cloning animals, but he continues to use genetic engineering for medical research.

frequently overlooked. The scientists who cloned Dolly were interested in making transgenic animals to produce vaccines and other useful human proteins. Scientists hoped that cloning would provide a way of producing large numbers of identical transgenic animals that could produce much-needed human proteins.

Dolly was the first successful clone, but she was not a transgenic animal. After the success of cloning Dolly, researchers went on to produce other cloned animals, including some transgenic animals that produced useful proteins in their milk.

Researchers have had some successes, but as more clones are produced, problems with the cloning technique have also become clear. The success rate for cloning is low: Fewer than one clone in one hundred survives to birth. Also, evidence shows that even successful clones are damaged in some way during the cloning process, and clones age more quickly than normal animals. Dolly grew to adulthood and produced lambs, but she became seriously ill. Cloned animals tend to die young. The reasons for the short lives of cloned animals are not fully understood at this time.

Dolly the sheep lived almost seven years and gave birth to four lambs through natural breeding processes. In early 2003, her owners discovered that she had developed a progressive lung disease and was euthanized ("put down"). Sheep normally live eleven to twelve years.

Cloning success

Cloning poses problems, but it is still a good way to produce transgenic animals. Transgenic animals can then be bred in the normal way. Genes are passed from parents to their offspring as Mendel originally described (*see pages 14–17*). As a result, some offspring do not inherit the transgenic gene from their mother while others do. A herd of transgenic animals can therefore be produced over time by using normal breeding techniques.

Currently, several herds of transgenic animals produce a number of different proteins. One herd of goats, on a farm in Charlton, Massachusetts, produces a protein called antithrombin III, which reduces blood clotting. Researchers hope that the transgenic proteins from the milk of these goats will soon help save lives.

This photo shows part of the process of cloning a mouse by nuclear transfer. A pipette (*on the left*) holds a mouse egg cell in place. The egg nucleus has been removed, and a nucleus from an adult cell is being injected through a needle (*on the right*).

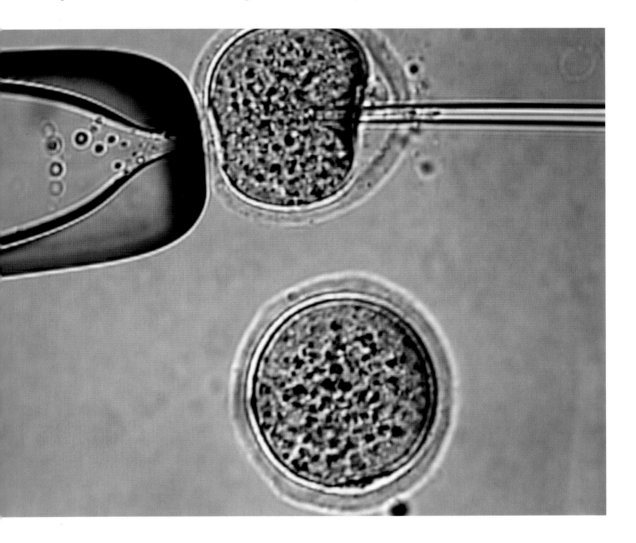

A cloned human?

We have cloned many mammals—could we clone a human? Most scientists say that cloning humans is far too risky. Judging from experiences with animal cloning, a human cloned using available techniques would have less than a one-in-one-hundred chance of surviving. A cloned human would perhaps grow to adulthood, but it would have a short life, as Dolly did. Present cloning techniques place human cloning solidly in the realm of science fiction.

CUTTING EDGE   FACTS

Cloning time line

1901	In Germany, Hans Spemann split a two-cell newt embryo in half, and two complete larvae developed.
1952	U.S. researchers Robert Briggs and Thomas J. King clone frogs by removing the nuclei from early embryos and placing them into enucleated egg cells.
1975	British scientist J. Derek Bromhall clones a rabbit using a similar technique to that used for frogs.
1986	Danish scientist Steen Willadsen, working in Britain, discovers that an electric shock fuses the nucleus of a sheep embryo with an enucleated egg cell (one that has had its nucleus removed). Using this technique, he clones a sheep. This is an advance from making clones by splitting an early embryo; it lays the groundwork for Dolly.
1996	In Scotland, Ian Wilmut and colleagues clone Dolly the sheep, the first mammal cloned using DNA from an adult animal.
1997	In the U.S., Don Wolf and colleagues clone a rhesus monkey using the same techniques that were used for cloning Dolly. Ian Wilmut's team clones Polly, the transgenic sheep.
1998	U.S. researchers Richard Seed and Lee Bo-yen claim to have cloned a human egg and grown it to the four-cell stage. (Claims not proved.)
1999	Japanese scientists Tenuhiko Wakayama and Ryuzo Yanagumachi clone a male mouse—the first male mammal cloned from adult cells.
2002	U.S. Congress bans human cloning research.
2005	In South Korea, Woo-Suk Hwang and his team clone the first dog. Dogs have proved particularly hard to clone.

Xenotransplantation

The goats, sheep, and cows being produced for their special milk are not the only transgenic animals that researchers are developing. Transgenic pigs are being developed so that their organs can be transplanted into people. Transplantation of cells, tissues, or organs between species is a xenograft, or xenotransplantation.

Xenotransplantation might seem like science fiction, but it has occurred since the 1960s. Many people with bad heart valves owe their lives to a porcine (pig) heart valve implant. All over the world, seriously ill people need whole organs, such as hearts, kidneys, livers, and lungs. Unfortunately, not enough donor organs are available for everyone who needs them. For instance, in the U.S. alone, seventy thousand people are waiting for donor organs.

The organs of a pig are about the same size as those of a human, so they could, in theory, be used for xenotransplants. Some experimental transplants have been made, but there is a stumbling block: organ rejection.

CUTTING EDGE   DEBATES

The xenotransplant debate

Although many people feel that xenotransplants may, in the future, provide whole organs for transplant surgery, others are strongly against such procedures. Despite several attempts in the past twenty-five years, no whole-organ xenotransplants have succeeded. Researchers have yet to overcome the problem of rejection of nonhuman organs. (All pig cells are "washed" from the valves used to replace human heart valves.) The inadvertant transfer of a nonhuman virus to the organ recipient poses another serious concern regarding xenotranplants.

"Me" or "not me"

A patient who receives a transplanted organ faces the possibility that his or her body will reject the organ. Rejection occurs when the immune system—the body system that defends against diseases—recognizes that the new organ is "not me." Any material (except for food) introduced into the body from another animal—even from another human—alerts the body's immune system. A rejection reaction harms the transplanted tissue and can kill the patient.

Antigens appear as red
bodies on the surface
of a cell in this computer-
generated image.

An activated immune system sends out white blood cells (WBCs) that engulf and destroy harmful substances. Antibodies carried by WBCs identify cells as "not self" because of the natural "label" on the outside of every cell. The cells of every individual carry unique antibodies—only the antibodies of identical twins are a match. The antibody found on any foreign cell is called an antigen.

Transplant rejection

A recipient's immune system identifies the "new" organ as "not me" because of the antigens carried by the donor organ. The immune response focuses mobilizing its WBCs into attacking the "invader" and rejecting the organ. The larger the difference between donor and recipient, the stronger the attack.

Doctors who perform transplants must use organs with tissues and blood type as similar as possible to those of the patient. Organ recipients also receive drugs called immunosuppressants to prevent the immune system from rejecting the transplanted organ.

Genetically engineered pigs

In addition to antigens, pig cells carry other chemicals on their surfaces that cause severe immune reactions. Because of these chemicals, a normal pig organ would be rejected within hours of transplantation into a human. To solve this problem, researchers have produced genetically engineered pigs whose cells do not carry such chemicals. While this advances the prospects of using pig organs in xenotransplants, it does not solve the antigen problem. Further genetic engineering changes must be made before pig organs can be transplanted into humans without rejection.

Problem viruses?

Every species of animal has some viruses that are actually incorporated into the DNA of that animal, and these viruses live inside its cells. No research has ever shown that pig viruses were transferred to a human through organ transplants.

CUTTING EDGE MOMENTS

Bridging the gap

In 1997, Briton Robert Pennington nearly died of liver failure. Doctors hoped to perform a liver transplant, but no suitable donor organ was available. In order to keep him alive as they continued to search for a donor liver, surgeons diverted Pennington's blood through the liver of a transgenic pig. After three days, they located a liver suitable for transplant. It marked the first time an animal organ kept someone waiting for a transplant alive until a donor organ became available.

Chimeras

A chimera is an animal made partly of one animal and partly of another. For example, a goat bred with a sheep is a chimera (*see image and caption, this page*). Some researchers are investigating whether chimeras that include some human cells could serve as organ donors for transplant patients.

To make a chimera with human cells, researchers would inject human cells from culture (grown in a laboratory) into an animal embryo inside its mother's uterus. At this stage of its life, the embryo's immune system is not working, so the foreign (human) cells are not rejected. The human cells would grow and divide along with the embryo's other tissues. The chimera embryo would grow into an animal fetus with patches of human tissue among that animal's normal body cells.

At present, researchers cannot control where the human cells in a chimera might appear. In the future, it may be possible to produce chimeras that have one or more complete, working organs made of human cells. Chimeras pose a special ethical problem for many people: Even if the research improves human health, is it morally right to use genetic engineering techniques to produce new kinds of animals simply for the benefit of humans?

A chimera is made by combining cells from the embryos of two different animals. The chimera shown here was produced by the union of a goat embryo and a sheep embryo. Its coat has areas of sheep wool and areas of goat hair. Such research remains controversial and poses an enormous array of ethical questions. Many times, the animals used in genetic research do not live very long, and the quality of their lives may not match normal expectations. Animal rights proponents may also question whether or not researchers who create chimeras are "playing God" by experimenting on living, feeling creatures.

45

CHAPTER 6

Stem Cells

The birth of Dolly the sheep sparked a huge interest in cloning. Several laboratories claimed to be close to cloning a human, which started a fierce public debate. Should we clone humans or not? People react strongly to the idea of human cloning. It not only goes against many religious beliefs, but also raises the questions of the great risks involved in the cloning process.

Most researchers working in the field of cloning are not interested in producing cloned human babies. They focus their research on another, more practical type of cloning—therapeutic cloning. The goal of therapeutic cloning is to grow human embryos to the blastocyst stage. A blastocyst is a ball of cells with a cavity in the center. Inside is an inner cell mass consisting of a layer of "undifferentiated" stem cells. These cells are not yet "programmed" to develop into a specific type of body cell, such as a muscle or a nerve cell. Because stem cells have the potential to grow into any type of cell, they not only could help solve the problem of organ rejection in transplants, but also could provide treatments for other conditions.

Stem cells uses

At a certain stage of development, most cells in the human body become specialized and develop into specific types of cells. For instance, cells that become nerve cells grow long, thin extensions that can transmit electrical impulses within the body. Cells destined to form muscles usually assume a spindle shape and develop the ability to contract (shorten).

CUTTING EDGE   SCIENCE

Immortal cells

Like the CHO stem cells (*see page 24*), certain stem cell lines seem to be immortal (they continue dividing indefinitely). Human stem cells, however, grow slowly and are difficult to keep alive in culture.

Specialized cells form through normal cell division. For example, cells that form the liver can never change into bone cells. The liver, however, contains a number of stem cells that retain the ability to grow, renew, and repair the liver itself. In fact, each body tissue includes groups of stem cells that function as biological repair kits.

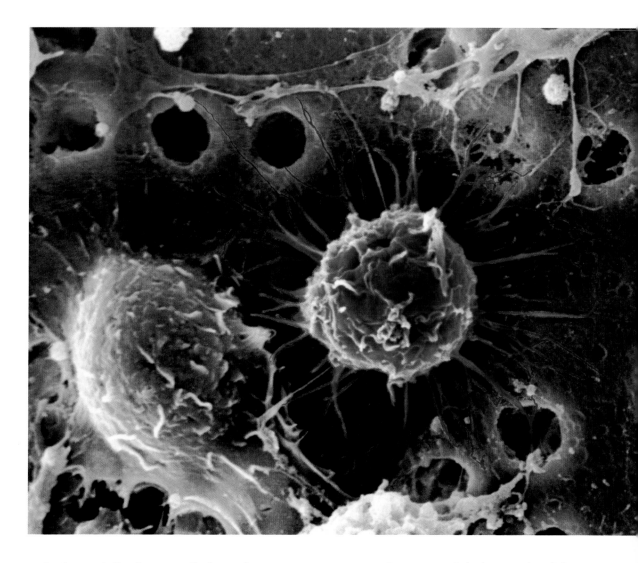

Such specialized stem cells keep the tissues in a person's body working properly and help keep that person healthy. Stem cells from the liver have "differentiated" to function only in the liver; likewise, stem cells from the lungs only function in the lungs. While some research targets these differentiated stem cells, most of the stem cell research that makes the news involves the undifferentiated stem cells in the early embryo's blastocyst stage.

Body tissues produce their own sets of stem cells to keep that tissue healthy. The purple cell on the right is a bone marrow stem cell.

47

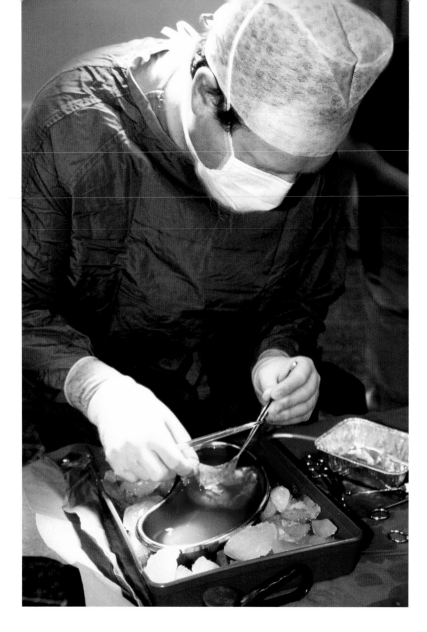

A doctor prepares a donor kidney prior to transplant. Although a kidney transplant is a fairly simple operation, donor kidneys are not readily available for all the patients who need them. Researchers hope that stem cell research will someday make it possible to grow new kidneys from stem cells.

Embryonic stem cells

Stem cells from embryos are different from adult stem cells. Adult stem cells divide and specialize. Embryonic stem cells, however, can become any kind of body cell or tissue. Researchers are interested in the enormous medical potential of embryonic stem cells. For instance, embryonic stem cells could help regrow damaged nerves in people who are paralyzed because of a spinal cord injury. Embryonic stem cells could also produce insulin in people with diabetes (*see page 23*).

In the future, researchers hope to develop a process to grow completely new organs for use in transplant surgery from embryonic stem cells. Organs grown from embryonic stem cells would still cause rejection problems for the organ recipient, however. (*see pages 42–43*). Much current stem cell research focuses on solving tissue rejection reactions in transplant patients.

Cloning stem cells

The best way to avoid a stem-cell rejection reaction is to use therapeutic cloning to produce stem cells with the same genetic makeup as the patient. Therapeutic cloning employs the same basic technique as that used to clone Dolly. A nucleus from one of the patient's own cells could be inserted into a human egg cell. The egg would be allowed to grow until embryonic stem cells formed. Researchers would "engineer" these "therapeutic" stem cells into forming the desired tissues or organs. The resulting tissues would contain not only the same DNA, but also the surface antigens of the new tissues would match those of other body cells of the patient and eliminate the danger of rejection.

Successes and setbacks

Although therapeutic cloning holds much promise for treating a variety of diseases, researchers are still a long way from being able to successfully clone stem cells. In November 2001, researchers in Worchester, Massachusetts, inserted a nucleus from an adult body cell into an enucleated egg. The resulting combination began dividing, but the egg cell did not divide for long enough time to reach the stage that produces stem cells. It stopped growing after reaching the six-cell stage.

In 2004, South Korean researchers caused a worldwide stir when they reported that they had successfully created human stem cells. An investigation in 2006 revealed that the South Korean research results were falsifed (*see panel on page 51*). The discredited research caused a serious setback for the field of stem cell research.

CUTTING EDGE **SCIENCE**

Stem cell therapy

Recent research has suggested that a patient's own stem cells can help treat some kinds of illness. Lupus erythematosus is a life-threatening disorder in which the body's immune system attacks its own body tissues. A new treatment for lupus involves removing a sample of stem cells from the patient's bone marrow and storing them. (Bone marrow stem cells produce the white blood cells—the key cells of the body's immune system.) After removal of the bone marrow stem cells, the patient undergoes treatment with a mixture of medications that destroys his or her immune system. The original bone marrow stem cells are then transfused back into the patient. In theory, the stem cells should rebuild the patient's immune system from scratch.

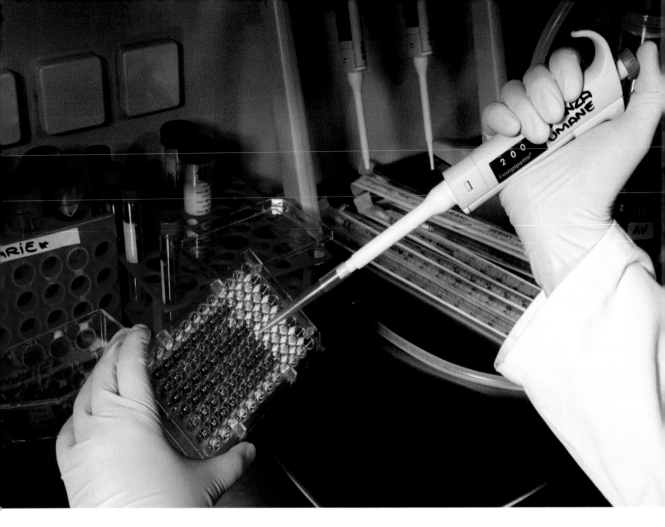

Stem cell lines

Developing a number of different stem cell types (known as "cell lines") is another way to avoid stem cell rejection. Researchers hope to develop cell cultures made from at least one thousand genetically different cell lines. Because embryonic stem cells are "immortal" (*see sidebar, page 46*), each stem cell line could keep dividing indefinitely in the laboratory. Such a large number of cell lines should make it possible to find a close genetic match for any patient needing new tissues or organs. Although each type of stem cell would not exactly match an individual patient, the match would be close enough to allow the use of those stem cells—in combination with drugs that suppress the immune system. It would also elminate the effects of major organ rejection.

At present, stem cells cannot be grown from unfertilized eggs by replacing the nucleus. Another technique, however, does work. Doctors take two unfertilized eggs from the same woman, remove the genetic material from one egg, and add it to the other. The egg

A researcher uses a micropipette to conduct experiments on stem cells. The special pipette delivers minute amounts of different concentrations of chemicals to each individual compartment of the array holding the stem cells. Embryonic stem cells can be stimulated to "differentiate," or develop, into any kind of body tissue or organ.

now has double its normal number of genes. (Remember: Gametes contain only half the number of genes of a normal cell). An unfertilized egg with double the number of genes has the correct amount of genes to develop normally. Researchers initiate cell division in the modified egg cell with a tiny electric shock.

Ethical issues

Many people justify embryonic stem cell research because therapeutic cloning holds much promise for treatment or cure of many debilitating (very serious) diseases. Others oppose such research because it involves tampering with, and destroying, embryos that could potentially develop into human beings. They also fear that it could lead to the cloning of human babies.

For these reasons, the U.S. government has opposed funding stem cell research. Some U.S. scientists instead concentrate on isolating different adult stem cells. They hope to use GE techniques to make such cells medically useful. Other researchers experienced limited success with using a patient's own stem cells to treat some diseases (*see sidebar, page 49*), but so far, genetically modified adult stem cells are not medically useful. Another groundbreaking technique involves taking only one cell from an embryo for culturing—which does not destroy the embryo. This research is so new that very little data exists to say whether or not it will succeed.

CUTTING EDGE MOMENTS

Faking the results

In January 2006, a public investigation into the work of South Korean scientist Woo-Suk Hwang revealed that he falsified the results of two stem cell studies. In these studies he claimed to have inserted DNA from adults into human egg cells, grown the eggs to blastocyst stage, and harvested the stem cells. The investigation found that the photographs and other evidence for the human research were false. Hwang's earlier achievement of cloning the first dog was authentic, however, so he was obviously capable of high-quality research work. What would make a respected scientist do such a thing? The most likely explanation is that Hwang falsified his results in order to maintain his high status in Korea and to ensure that his research continued to receive funding.

CHAPTER 7

Combating Aging

Most people hope to live a long, healthy life. Today, people in developed countries generally live longer than those in developing countries. Better nutrition, a higher standard of living, and improved health care contribute to increased longevity. Genetic engineering offers the possibility of making aging a healthier experience. It may add years to the average life span.

Evolution and aging

Some evidence suggests that people age because of natural selection. Natural selection is often called "survival of the fittest." It is the process by which the individuals best suited to a particular environment survive to reproduce and pass on their genes. Genes that cause illness are weeded out of the gene pool because people who have genetic disorders are less likely to survive and reproduce. Once people have reproduced and brought up children, natural selection ceases to operate: Staying fit and strong is no longer an advantage. Natural selection might therefore "dictate" that we age and die.

Evidence suggests that staying fit helps people survive. People who eat well and exercise regularly throughout their lives are likely to remain healthy as they age.

Longevity genes

Experiments with fruit flies suggests that natural selection has an effect on aging. Scientists at the University of California, Irvine found that they could lengthen the lives of fruit flies live by delaying the age at which they reproduced.

From these experiments and research using other animals, genetic researchers identified a number of "longevity genes" that are connected to living longer. Many of these genes help an animal combat environmental stresses, such as harmful chemicals or radiation, that can cause mutations. Longevity genes also affect the body's immune system and its genetic-repair mechanisms. In the case of the long-lived fruit flies, the longevity gene (named the Methuselah gene) acted by preventing cells from self-destructing when under stress.

Perhaps the most promising longevity gene is called SIR2. This gene was originally identified in yeasts and worms, but humans have a version, too. Stress activates the SIR2 gene. One of its effects may be to stop cells from self-destructing when they become stressed. Over time, cell destruction causes aging.

CUTTING EDGE   FACTS

Longevity genes
Several genes (or the proteins they produce) that affect life span are listed in the table below.

Gene or protein	Organism	Amount of increase in life span	Must gene or protein increase or decrease its production?	Effect(s) of gene or protein
SIR2	yeast, worm, fly	30 percent	increase production	stops cells from self-destructing under stress
daf-2	worm, fly, mouse	100 percent live twice as long	decrease production	growth and breakdown of food for energy
Growth hormone	Mouse, rat	7 to 150 percent, depending on levels of hormone	decrease production	regulates body size
Catalase (CAT)	mouse	20 percent	increase production	reduces free radicals (*see pages 54–55*)
Klotho	mouse	18 to 31 percent	increase production	regulates some hormones and parts of the immune system
Methuselah (CD97)	fly	35 percent	decrease production	stops cells from self-destructing under stress and improves communication between nerve cells

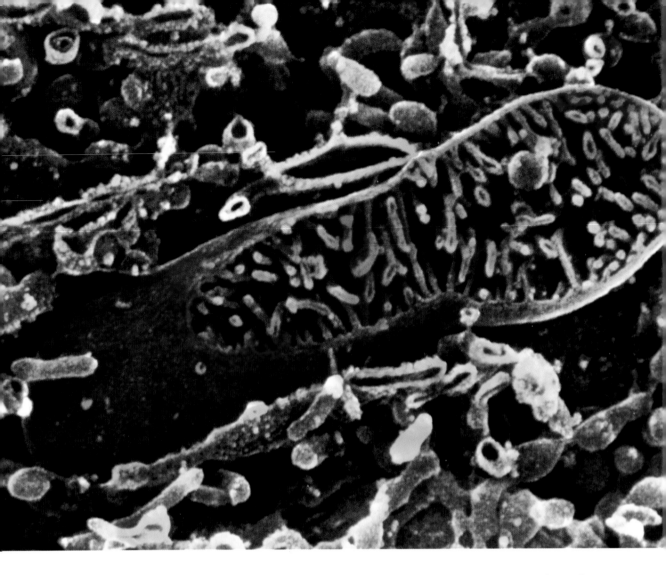

Genes in the energy factories

Another promising line of research into aging focuses on substances called free radicals. Free radicals are destructive chemicals that can damage DNA, proteins, or other large, complex molecules found in cells. Fruit flies bred to develop supercharged defenses against free radicals live significantly longer than normal.

Recent research on mice suggests that the main effects of free radicals occur in mitochondria. Mitochondria are the energy factories of cells. They break down the nutrients from food and produce the metabolic energy used by the body. The energy-production process requires oxygen, and any mistakes or interruptions can cause free radicals to form.

Although 99 percent of DNA is found in the nucleus of a cell, mitochondria also contain small amounts of DNA. Mitochondrial DNA codes for proteins involved in energy production. The free

An electronmicrograph shows a mitochondrion from an intestinal cell. Mitochondria power cell metabolism. Doctors think that damage to mitochondrial DNA may be a major cause of aging.

radicals that sometimes form during energy production can damage mitochondrial DNA. Body cells have defenses to protect mitochondrial DNA, but it is still more likely to be damaged by free radicals than the genetic material in the nucleus. Mitochondria with damaged DNA do not work properly. When enough mitochondria are damaged, cells begin to die—which causes aging.

Researchers are looking at ways of improving the life span of mitochondria by boosting the cellular defenses against free radicals. Compounds such as vitamin C and vitamin E function as antioxidants. Both occur naturally in foods and are plentiful in a healthy diet. These compounds can change free radicals and make them harmless. As yet, however, we cannot increase the activity of antioxidants in the places where they are needed.

Do we want to live longer?

People in developed countries already live longer, healthier lives than in the past. If this trend continues, humans will face some new challenges. Slightly more than six billion people populate the world. If individuals live longer, the population will rise further. How will we feed and house everyone? If people live longer, will they also be healthier in old age? If not, the medical costs for the large numbers of older people will become very high. Finally, if people live longer, when should they retire? It will no longer be possible for people to retire at the traditional ages of sixty or sixty-five, because it will cost too much to pay pensions to people for the thirty or forty years of life left to them after they retire.

CUTTING EDGE   SCIENCE

Guaranteed to lengthen life

For more than seventy years, researchers have known that a restricted-calorie diet seems to protect against many illnesses and prolong life. Animals fed 30 to 40 percent fewer calories than their normal diet throughout their lives live longer, healthier lives. Researchers discovered that the restricted-calorie diet positively affects the developing immune system, making it more efficient. No long-term data exists for humans (not many people want to purposely starve themselves for long periods), but short-term tests support the improved-health findings.

CHAPTER 8

The Future of Genetic Engineering

Researchers have made some remarkable advances in the field of genetics over the past few decades. They know the sequence of bases of the entire human genome, and thousands of genes have been identified. Geneticists can extract genes from human DNA and make many copies of them. They can splice genes into microbes or into cell cultures to make protein factories. They can remove all the genes from one animal, put them in an egg cell of another animal, and grow them successfully.

Practical medical applications for these genetic advances, however, remain limited. Although we understand the causes of and can test for many genetic disorders, and can manufacture many medically useful human proteins through genetic engineering, genetics is still in its infancy. Genetic sciences stand on the verge of a revolution that could transform medicine.

CUTTING EDGE   SCIENCE

What about RNA?

In 1993, researchers discovered that RNA plays a more significant role in cell metabolism than simply copying and transporting the gene codes stored in DNA and then synthesizing proteins from them. Smaller sections of RNA called microRNA (miRNA) help regulate genetic activity, such as turning genes "on" and "off." Other research links miRNA to tumor growth and hints that doctors may someday "read" a patient's miRNA to predict not only if a person will develop cancer, but also what type of cancer. So far, researchers have identified at least two hundred types of miRNA, but do not know for certain how many thousands of types of miRNA may exist. In fact, one researcher compared miRNA to the "dark matter" of the universe.

An amazing repair kit

Stem cells are likely to spearhead this revolution. Techniques for incorporating a patient's DNA into stem cells must be perfected, and researchers need to find out how to control stem cell development. Once doctors overcome these problems, they will have access to an enormously powerful body repair kit. Stem cells could be grown into new nerves, muscles, bones, or other tissues to repair damage caused by accidents or illnesses.

Researchers have already successfully grown organs from patients' own cells on frameworks of protein fibers. They may soon use this technique to grow organs from stem cells. Emerging technology might even allow researchers to "print" new organs! Modified inkjet printers are already used to lay down layers of living cells in a gel that becomes solid when warmed. If this technology is combined with stem cells, organ printing might become a reality.

The colored bands below show some of the three billion base pairs that make up the genetic code of human DNA. Each colored band represents the position of one of the four nucleotide bases that forms the genetic code. As researchers learn more about what each part of DNA does, their ability to incorporate genetics in medicine will improve.

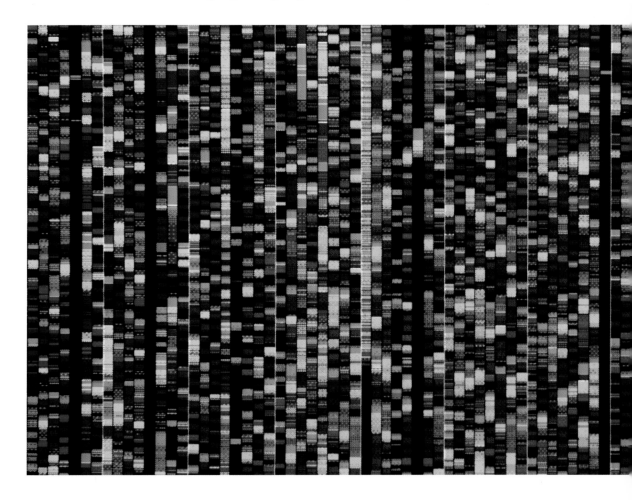

Gene therapy

We have yet to develop the tools that will precisely deliver replacement genes to body areas that need them—and that will "turn on" once they reach their destination. Such advances in gene therapy would revolutionize medicine by offering treatments or even cures for a range of genetic disorders, including Alzheimer's disease, sickle cell disease, Down syndrome, and many others.

A computer-generated image shows cloned babies. Genetic researchers have not cloned humans. If parents could one day choose some of their children's characteristics or clone their children, should they do so?

Genetic smart cards

DNA microarrays make possible quick and easy genetic testing. Doctors in the near future may test and record a newborn's genome (DNA) upon delivery. Knowledge of genetic disorders and weaknesses should someday make it possible for people to improve their health. Doctors could study their patients' DNA and advise them on how to avoid health risks.

People may someday carry around a copy of their genome on a "smart card." The smart card would provide information that doctors could use to tailor treatment for each individual (*see sidebar, below*). Knowing the genome of a fetus could also someday help doctors identify and correct genetic disorders before birth.

CUTTING EDGE — SCIENCE

Tailor-made treatment

The more we know about an individual's genome, the more doctors can "tailor" treatment to match that individual. Heart disease, for instance, takes many different forms. Although doctors can easily diagnose heart disease, finding the underlying cause is not always a straightforward process. A lack of exercise and poor diet can cause heart disease, but genetic disorders can also affect the heart. If a doctor knows that a patient has a specific gene allele, the doctor can offer treatment targeted to that form of the disease.

Controlling genetics

The swift advances in medical genetics presents some tough questions. Is it acceptable to obtain stem cells by destroying embryos that could grow into humans? What if those embryos would be discarded anyway? Is it right to use other animal species for genetic experiments if the procedures may sometimes harm those animals? If altering the genome of a fetus will avoid the development of a genetic disease later in life, should it occur? How can we prevent "DNA discrimination" by health insurance companies and protect the confidentiality of an individual's genetic information? Should human cloning be allowed? As scientists develop advanced medical genetic techniques, societies must decide how to put such knowledge to the best use possible.

Glossary

allele A particular version of a gene.

amino acids The raw materials that join together to make a protein.

antibody A protein produced by white blood cells that help fight diseases by recognizing "foreign" microbes.

antigen A microbe, harmful chemical, or other substance that stimulates a host's immune system to produce antibodies.

bacteria Microscopic, primitive single-celled living organisms whose DNA is scattered throughout the cell instead of contained within the nucleus.

catalyst A substance that affects a chemical reaction but does not enter into the reaction.

cell culture Human or other animal cells that are grown in a laboratory.

chromosome A long chain of genetic material (DNA) that forms in the cell nucleus during cell division.

clone An exact genetic copy of another living thing. Identical twins are clones.

DNA (deoxyribonucleic acid) The genetic material that contains all the information needed to make an organism.

dominant trait The (usually) physical characteristic displayed in an offspring caused by the inheritance of a gene carried by only one parent (*see recessive trait*).

embryo A very early stage of development of a human or animal.

enzymes Proteins that speed up the chemical reactions that are essential to life.

evolution The gradual biological changes over time in plants or animals caused by changes in the DNA of those organisms.

fermenter A large container for bacteria or other microbes that is used for large-scale production of proteins from genetically modified microbes.

fluorescent A material that glows in the dark.

gamete An egg or sperm cell that contains one-half the genetic information of its parent.

gene A section of DNA that carries the code to produce a protein or a group of proteins.

gene pool The possible combinations of genes available to a breeding pair of organisms.

gene therapy Treatment for a genetic disorder that involves giving the patient a corrected copy of the damaged gene that causes the disorder.

genetic disorder A disease or illness caused by a gene that does not work properly or is different from normal.

genetic engineering Using genetic techniques to change the DNA of an animal or plant.

genetics The study of how genes affect metabolism, diseases, and reproduction.

genome The set of genes that contain the DNA codes to create a particular organism.

genotype The genetic code that causes a specifc characteristic.

hemophilia A genetic disorder of the blood in which the blood does not clot properly.

heredity The set of genes and characteristics passed from one generation to the next.

hormone A natural chemical "messenger" that travels through the bloodstream to affect cells.

immune system The body's defense system against disease and injury.

mammal A warm-blooded animal, usually hairy or furry, feed on breast milk when young.

messenger RNA (mRNA) A material that copies genetic information from the nucleus and carries it to the ribosomes in the cytoplasm.

mutation A change in the sequence of bases along a DNA molecule, produced by exposure to radiation, chemicals, or some other factor.

natural selection The process by which those individuals most suited to an environment survive and reproduce.

nucleotide One of the linked subunits consisting of a sugar, a phospate, and a base that make up DNA or RNA.

nucleus The control center of a cell.

phenotype The physical characteristics of a plant or animal that develop because of genes.

platelets Small, disk-like blood cell fragments that are important for blood clotting.

proteins An important group of substances that form structures such as skin, hair, and muscle and that also control processes inside cells.

recessive trait A (usually) physical characteristic that does not appear in offspring unless it is inherited within genes from both parents (*see dominant trait*).

rejection An immune system reaction that attacks a transplanted organ or tissue, causing major metabolic problems that can "kill" the transplant and host.

ribosome An organelle in the cytoplasm that is the site for protein production.

RNA (ribonucleic acid) A single-stranded substance similar to DNA that carries genetic information from the nucleus to cytoplasm and can direct other cellular processes.

sequencing The determination of the order of bases along a DNA molecule.

stem cells Undifferentiated (non-specialized) cells that have the potential to divide and develop into many different kinds of cells.

transgenic animal A genetically modified animal that carries genes from another organism.

ultraviolet An invisible wavelength of light on the shorter end of the electromagnetic spectrum.

vaccine A substance that stimulates the immune system to produce antibodies against a disease.

virus A very simple living organism that has no DNA of its own but reproduces by invading the nuclei in the cells of other organisms.

xenotransplantation Transplanting organ, tissues, or cells from one species into another.

yeast A tiny, single-celled microbe that is a type of fungus. Yeasts are used for making bread, beer, and wine. They can also cause infections.

Further Information

BOOKS

Bankston, John. *Gregor Mendel and the Discovery of the Gene.* Uncharted, Unexplored, and Unexplained: Scientific Advancements of the 19th Century (series). Mitchell Lane Publishers (2004).

Bédoyère, Camilla de la. *The Discovery of DNA.* Milestones In Modern Science (series). World Almanac® Library (2006).

Dowswell, Paul. *Genetic Engineering*: 21st Century Issues (series). World Almanac® Library (2005).

Graham, Ian. *Genetics: The Study of Heredity.* Investigating Science (series). Gareth Stevens Publishing (2002).

Macdonald, Fiona. *The First "Test Tube Baby."* Days That Changed the World (series). World Almanac® Library (2004).

Woolf, Alex. *History of Medicine: Medicine in the Twentieth Century and Beyond.* Enchanted Lion Books (2006).

WEB SITES

www.dnaftb.org/dnaftb/
Learn about genetics through an easy-to-read, animated Web site.

doegenomes.org/
Discover the latest genetic research programs sponsored by the U.S. government.

www.ornl.gov/sci/techresources/Human_Genome/project/info.shtml
Follow the links for basic information about genetics and the human genome project.

www.sciencemuseum.org.uk/antenna/dolly/index.asp
Read the Science Museum of London's overview of Dolly the sheep's life.

sickle.bwh.harvard.edu/menu_sickle.html
Find out more about the first genetic disorder identified on a molecular basis.

www.genetics.gsk.com/kids/index_kids.htm
Visit the Glaxosmithkline Web site and follow the links for fascinating information.

Index

Index *(continued)*